Romantic Fantasies

Gregory J.P. Godek

bestselling author of *1001 Ways to Be Romantic*

CASABLANCA PRESS
A DIVISION OF SOURCEBOOKS
NAPERVILLE, IL

Published by: Sourcebooks, Inc.
P.O. Box 372, Naperville, Illinois 60566
(630) 961-3900
FAX: (630) 961-2168

Cover design by Scott Theisen
Internal design and production by Andrew Sardina, Scott Theisen
and Joe Leamon

*D*edication

*To everyone who keeps mystery and fantasy alive in
the world and in their own relationships.*

*And, of course, to my Bride, Tracey—my own magical
manifestation of fantasy and reality.*

Library of Congress Cataloging-in-Publication Date
Godek, Gregory J.P.
        Romantic fantasies / by Gregory J.P. Godek.
              p.   cm.
        "A Casablanca book"
        ISBN 1-57071-154-2
        1. Sexual fantasies.   2. Sexual excitement.   3. Sex.   I. Title.
HQ21.G597   1997
306.7–dc21   96-52852
                                                                 CIP

Printed and bound in the United States of America.

10 9 8 7 6 5 4 3 2 1

Contents

Introduction v

Arousal 1

Awakening Your Senses 6

Boys Will Be Boys 11

Celebrate! 14

Creativity 17

Dressing Up 22

Ecstasy 24

Express Yourself 30

Fantasies 35

Food, Glorious Food 39

Fun & Games 45

Girl Talk 49

Honeymoon 52

Hot! 55

Imagination 58

Le Boudoir 62

Lingerie 66

Lovemaking 71

Variety 73

Mindset of a Sex Maniac 76

Sexy Stuff 80

Orgasm 84

Outrageous 86

Questions 90

Role Playing 93

Seduction 96

Sex in the Movies 96

Sex, Sex, Sex 99

Sexy Songs 103

More Sexy Stuff 106

Taking Care of Business 109

Time for Sex 113

ABCs of Sex 117

Introduction

*W*elcome to the world of romantic fantasy. A place where we explore the sexy side of love. A place where imagination runs wild. A place of love and a place of passion.

Love, romance and sex—while different and distinct—are inextricably intertwined. They sometimes seem to stand alone, but in reality it is simply one or another of them taking center stage for a brief moment. The interplay of the three of them is what makes a relationship fascinating, unpredictable, joyful and meaningful.

My belief is that love, romance and sex are each enhanced by the others. Thus, to overemphasize any one of them threatens to unbalance the equation. That's why this book links sex very closely with romance, creativity, a little craziness and a lot of trust.

This certainly isn't a sex manual (that's Dr. Ruth's job). It's a collection of old and new ideas—from the *1001 Ways to Be Romantic* series of books, from my seminars, and from my readers—all designed to help you, challenge you, excite you and reignite the passion in your relationship.

This book is a resource, a reminder, and an inspiration that I hope you will carry with you long after you've misplaced this book or passed it on to someone you care about.

Gregory J.P. Godek

January 1997

Arousal

*arouse—to stimulate, kindle, fire, animate, inspire,
incite, provoke, instigate.*

1

The subtleties of arousal ·

Let's talk about the subtleties of arousal—those very
personal feelings, passions, desires and fantasies that
we rarely talk about, even with our intimate partner.
We're not talking about direct sexual stimulation. We're
talking about erotic arousal, which involves more of
your senses, more of your body and more of your time.
The payoff is more satisfaction and deeper sexual intimacy. Let's explore what arouses you!

2

Homework: what arouses you?

- ❧ Get a pad and pen.
- ❧ List five things that turn you on.

- List five more.
- Have you ever shared these things with your lover?
- Do you arouse quickly or slowly?
- Are you aroused more by words? By visual stimulation? By music? By food? By specific clothing? By specific parts of your lover's body?

3

Your five senses

Which of your five senses is most sensitive? How are you aroused through this sense? Does your partner know this?

"Love is its own aphrodisiac and is the main ingredient for lasting sex."

~ *Mort Katz*

All-day foreplay

*H*ere's how you play: Decide first thing in the morning that you're going to make love with your partner this evening. Tease and flirt with him or her all day long—building up to the appointed time.

- Touch her provocatively before she gets out of bed in the morning.
- Shower together.
- Over breakfast, tell him that you slipped an aphrodisiac into his coffee.
- Hide a pair of your panties in his briefcase.
- Leave sexy messages on her voice mail.
- Send suggestive notes on his e-mail.
- Call her and whisper erotic thoughts during the day.
- In the evening, greet him at the door wearing your sexiest outfit.
- Have hot music playing on the stereo.
- Take a bubblebath together.
- Have dinner in bed.
- And last-but-not-least—have "dessert" in bed.

5
· · ·
Quickies!

 *T*here's nothing wrong with a little "quickie" now and then! Sometimes the lack of time for proper arousal is itself arousing!

———

Is there any difference between being aroused and simply being horny?

———

6
· · ·
If you had three hours...

 *T*he goal is to arouse your partner:

- ❧ How would you go about it if you had 10 minutes?
- ❧ How would you go about it if you had 30 minutes?
- ❧ How would you go about it if you had 1 hour?
- ❧ How would you go about it if you had 3 hours?
- ❧ How would you go about it if you had all day?
- ❧ How would you go about it if you had all weekend?

7

. . .

Role reversal

Try this little exercise for just 20 minutes, and you'll probably learn more about your partner than you've learned in the last 10 years.

Start foreplay, but each of you takes on the role of the other. Pay attention to how you touch each other; where you touch each other; how much time you take; how your partner responds.

After 20 minutes, stop! Talk about your experience; what you observed; what you learned. Now, switch back to your own role, and continue!

Awakening Your Senses

*While it's rather obvious that your sense of touch is integral
to sex, don't forget about your other four senses.
They can enhance your enjoyment of sex.*

8
. . .
Touch, see, hear, smell, taste

*I*n the process of getting to know one another, people
in new relationships tend to utilize all of their senses.
It's largely an unconscious thing. They touch one
another a lot; they snuggle close and smell the other's
unique odors; they gaze at one another; they listen to
one another; and they kiss and taste one another. The
use of all five senses helps you learn about the other
person, and it enhances, deepens and speeds the
process of building intimacy.

People in established relationships tend to fall into patterns of focusing on just one or two senses, and virtual-
ly ignoring the others. One way of getting "back in
touch" (pun intended) with your partner is to reintro-
duce the missing senses. An enhanced appreciation of

the senses parallels an enhanced appreciation of your lover.

9
. . .
Q&A

- ❧ What visually stimulates you?
- ❧ What aromas turn you on?
- ❧ What sounds make you horny?
- ❧ What tastes are erotic to you?
- ❧ What kind of touching is sexy to you?

10
. . .
Pitch black

Cover your bedroom windows well enough to make it absolutely pitch black at night.

- ❧ Make love in the dark.
- ❧ Make love in the dark without speaking at all.
- ❧ Make love in the dark with music on.

11

. . .

Playing "footsie"

*T*ry a little "foot reflexology." It's a form of foot massage based on the premise that there is a specific relationship between areas of the feet and other parts of the body. It can be extremely erotic. To get you started, read *The Complete Guide to Foot Reflexology*, by Kevin and Barbara Kunz.

12

. . .

Erotic communication

*U*se more than one sense in your erotic communications. Because our sense of smell is the most under-utilized sense, think up some ways of adding some sensuous aromas to your lover's life. Here's a start:

- Don't just send a love letter—send a scented love letter! Use your favorite cologne or perfume.
- Don't just hide some lingerie in his briefcase—add a dash of his favorite perfume.

13

. . .

A five-sense evening

*C*reate a "Five-Sense Evening," during which you and your lover stimulate all five of each other's senses. Enjoy!

14

. . .

Getting in touch with your body

*G*etting in touch with your own body will enhance your enjoyment of sex. Getting into better physical shape couldn't hurt. In addition, here are some specific methods that will enhance your body awareness:

- ❧ Dance. Modern. Tap. Ballroom. Whatever. Moving your body and working on your coordination will always benefit you.
- ❧ Yoga. Slowing down and limbering up.

- Martial arts. A little discipline never hurt anyone. You'll build self-confidence, too. Choose a technique that works for you.
- Feldenkrais. Take an "Awareness Through Movement" class. You'll be amazed that such subtle, gentle movements can change your body— and your mind!

15

The amateur masseuse

*M*ost of us are real amateurs when it comes to giving massages. Learn more from one of these books (and then practice, practice, practice!):

- *The Massage Book,* by George Downing
- *Massage: Principles & Techniques,* by Gertrude Beard & Elizabeth Wood

Boys Will Be Boys

16
* * *
A kiss is still a kiss

*J*ust thought you might like to know...the proper way
to kiss a woman's hand. Most men—even in the
movies—do it incorrectly. You're supposed to hold her
hand (gently but firmly) in a comfortable position
(comfortable for her, that is), and lower your lips to her
hand. DO NOT raise her hand to your lips.

17
* * *
Raging hormones!

*R*ecognize, capitalize on, and compensate for the
physiological differences between men and women that
affect lovemaking:
- Following orgasm, most men want to roll over and
  go to sleep...while most women are wide awake and

crave more intimacy. What to do? Well, you guys could realize that the chemical that makes you feel sleepy is effective for only a few minutes. If you can just wait-it-out, you'll feel awake and revitalized again!

🪰 Did you know that most men's hormone level is highest in the morning, while most women's is highest—you guessed it—in the evening?! (What a dirty trick!) It's just a fact of life. Compensate. Take turns. Be understanding.

> ## "The pillars of male identity are warfare, work and sex."
> ~ *Sam Keen*

18

Advice from a Victoria's Secret saleswoman

Here's some advice for you guys from a woman who used to work in a Victoria's Secret shop: "Please tell men to know their lady's bra size! It's not as simple as 'small,' 'medium,' and 'large'! I can't tell you how many men answer the question 'What bra size does she wear?' with 'About average,' or 'About as big as her,' they'll say, pointing to some poor embarrassed woman in the store."

19

G-spot

Go in search of her G-spot. You may not find it, but you'll have a great time looking! (You may want to pick up a copy of *The G-Spot,* by Alice Kahn Ladas, et al.)

20

Tit for tat

Guys, if you want your lover to wear lingerie more often, why do you think that you have the right to slouch around in your ratty boxer shorts or dirty sweat pants?! Take a hint! Get a nice bathrobe, or silk pajamas, or a lounging jacket, or a Japanese kimono.

Shave on Saturday night.

Celebrate!

- Celebrate Christmas: Wrap yourself up and wait for your lover underneath the Christmas tree.
- Celebrate Independence Day: Wrap yourself in a flag—and see if he salutes!
- Celebrate Halloween: Dress-up as a favorite fantasy character and treat each other to some great sex.
- Celebrate Thanksgiving: Give thanks for your relationship by giving sexual favors to your lover.
- Celebrate Groundhog Day: Go "underground": Take the day off work and stay in bed all day with your lover.

"Happy Anniversary—take off your clothes!"

*O*n your next anniversary, create a sexual gift or experience based on the number of years you've been married:

- ❧ On your 3rd anniversary—take a 3-day "Sexual Holiday."
- ❧ On your 10th anniversary—give her 10 "Orgasm Coupons."
- ❧ On your 22nd anniversary—give her 22 kisses—on 22 different body parts!

"There is only one happiness in life, to love and be loved."

~ George Sand

24

· · ·

Celebrating in your birthday suit

Celebrate your lover's next birthday with a sexy twist...

- ✤ Greet him at the front door wearing a big red ribbon—and nothing else.
- ✤ Write a sexy message on top of her birthday cake in frosting.
- ✤ Spend all day in your "birthday suits."

25

· · ·

Party on!

Celebrations and parties are great places for making love secretly! While at a party, slip away into a bedroom or private porch. While at a wedding reception, sneak away into a broom closet or restroom!

Creativity

26
. . .
Creativity counts

People with the most exciting sex lives are those who are creative in their sex lives! It's how they stay out of the rut that others fall into. It's how they stay interested. It's how they stay monogamous, too!

27
. . .
Learning and unlearning

Don't feel bad if you think you're not very creative. Chances are, you were never taught to be creative. Our educational system stresses facts and memorization over problem-solving and thinking skills.

The good news is that creativity can be taught—nourished, encouraged and unleashed! Actually, the process of "learning" creativity is more about *unlearning* habits that limit your thinking, than it is about learning new ideas. You were born creative. We're simply going to dip into the immense reservoir of creativity that's inside of you.

28
. . .
Creativity enhancers

- A playful attitude
- A belief that you're creative
- Ability to handle ambiguity
- Risk-taking
- Changing the rules
- Humor

Creativity blockers

- Following the rules
- Looking for one right answer
- Logical thinking
- Fear of failure
- Fear of embarrassment
- Belief that you're not creative

> "In order to create, there must be a dynamic force, and what force is more potent than love?"
>
> ~ *Igor Stravinsky*

29

Kitchen cuddling

*F*irst, let's apply a little creativity to *where* you make love. It's amazing how many people have never made love anywhere but in a bed! Try these locations to spice up your love life: In the bathtub, on the kitchen floor, on the dining room table, in the back yard, in an elevator, in a department store dressing room.

30
. . .

A change of pace

$\mathcal{N}$ext, let's apply a little creativity to the *timing* of how you make love. (Many people have never even thought about this aspect of lovemaking—they just go on automatic.) I'm not talking just about "fast" or "slow" (although that's a good place to start). I'm talking about changing pace to suit your lover's mood; about teasing; about ebbing and flowing.

- Spend *twice* as long on foreplay as you usually do.
- Linger on one part of your lover's body.
- Lightly lick your favorite part of your lover's body.
- Lightly lick your partner's favorite part of his/her body.

31
. . .

Zzzzzzz

$\mathcal{T}$iming also refers to when in the day you make love. Don't make the mistake of leaving it until everything else is done. By the end of the day, you'll simply be too exhausted.

32

Zip!

*T*ry making love as quickly as you possibly can. Time yourselves! Try to improve on your time every few months.

33

Going for the record

*T*ry making love for as long as you possibly can. Have you ever made love for an hour? Three hours? All afternoon? All day?All weekend?

34

Urban outfitters?

*C*reate or compile a sexy outfit. (In this case, we define "sexy outfit" as something that *your partner* finds outrageously sexy.)

Dressing Up

35
. . .
Here comes the bride

*G*als: Greet him at the front door wearing your wedding gown.

36
. . .
Tuxedo junction

*G*uys: Greet her some Tuesday evening wearing a tuxedo.

37
. . .
The masked lover strikes again!

*T*ake a little trip to a local costume shop. Use your imagination!

Romantic Fantasies

38
Lingerie shopping spree

Go on a five-minute shopping spree at Victoria's Secret. On your mark, get set...go!

Fantasy: A glimpse at our deeper desires—a creative exploration of our dreams.

~*Gregory J.P. Godek*

39
Rah!

How about that old cheerleader's uniform?!?

40

Follow the yellow brick road

*L*eave a trail of your clothes, leading from the front door to your bedroom.

Ecstasy

41

Whew!

*T*hink about the best sex, the hottest time, the most explosive orgasm you've ever had. Where were you? Who was your partner? What was the situation? How much time did you have? What were you wearing? What were you thinking?

(Whew!) Now, to the best of your ability—given the realities of your life right now—how can you recreate as many of the above circumstances as possible? Some

of the circumstances you will be able to recreate literally; some of them will have to be recreated in your imagination.

> "Only the united beat of sex and heart together can create ecstasy."
>
> ~ *Anais Nin*

42

. . .

Q&A

*D*o you *know* what your partner considers erotic? Or do you *assume* you know? Do you figure she likes what your last girlfriend enjoyed? Do you think he's just like the guy described in last month's *Cosmo*? Do you think all men are alike? Do you think all women are alike?

Set your inhibitions, judgments and timidness

aside…and talk about what each of you considers erotic. (Maybe warm-up with a little champagne.) Give yourselves plenty of time to explore this most amazing, complex and rewarding aspect of being human.

43

What's your "Sex Style"?

*W*hen it comes to making love/being sexy/expressing eroticism, what is your style? Do you stick to the "basics"? Are you creative? Are you wacky? Are you spontaneous? Do you have patterns? Are you verbal? Do you act out? Do you adjust your style based on your mood? Do you change based on your partner's mood?

In general, it's a good idea to focus on your natural style—on the things that fit your personality. However, don't stay stuck in your style. Experiment with a style that's a little foreign to you. Try a style that's the opposite of your natural style. It will stretch your repertoire, and your lover will probably appreciate an occasional change of pace.

44

. . .

Erotica

*E*rotica—The title of Madonna's 1992 album. This marked her return to the dance-driven numbers that first made her popular. One song is called "Deeper and Deeper." Uh-huh.

___

"Thou art to me a delicious torment."

~Ralph Waldo Emerson

___

45

. . .

The Erotic Mind

The Erotic Mind—The title of a book on eroticism and human sexuality that emphasizes the mind/body connection. By Jack Morin, M.D.

46

Positioning

Stretch your imagination. Exercise your options—and your body…try some new and exotic sexual positions.

47

Love & Lust—Erotic & Exotic

Discuss with your partner: What's the difference between "erotic" and "exotic"? What's the difference between "love" and "lust"?

48

S.W.A.K.

Don't forget about the simple but erotic pleasures of kissing. Too many of us have forgotten the excitement of lingering and probing kisses.

49
. . .
Read any good books lately?

*R*ead aloud to one another. Guys: She'll probably prefer the more "romantic" sex scenes. Gals: He'll probably prefer the more graphic, racy scenes. Some suggestions:

- *Delta of Venus,* by Anais Nin
- *Little Birds,* also by Anais Nin
- *Lady Chatterley's Lover,* by D.H. Lawrence
- *Tropic of Cancer,* by Henry Miller
- *Tropic of Capricorn,* also by Henry Miller
- *Yellow Silk,* edited by Lily Pond & Richard Russo

50
. . .
Experimenting

*O*ver the next three months, experiment by making love in a variety of different ways. Focus on one different way during each lovemaking session, and observe what you and your partner like best. Try these:

- Authoritatively
- Lustfully
- Sensually

- Roughly
- Publicly
- Quietly
- Loudly
- Innocently

Express Yourself

51

1-900-SEX-CALL

*C*all him at work in the middle of the day ...and explain in *explicit detail* how you're going to make love to him tonight. Tell him what you're going to wear, how you're going to touch him, what you're going to say to him. Then hang up!

52

Don't be shy

*H*ow do you communicate your desire to have sex

with your partner? Is it with a look? A gesture? How you dress? What you say? Are you subtle? Are you obvious?

Most people fall into a rut and use the same method all the time. Consider expanding your repertoire.

53

Once upon a time...

*W*rite a short, romantic, sexy story. One page long. Mail it to him at work.

54

. . .they lived happily ever after

*W*rite a short, romantic, sexy story. One page long. Mail it to him at work. When he comes home from work, act it out!

"When love and skill work together,
expect a masterpiece."

~ John Ruskin

55

Hmmmm

Rewrite the lyrics to her favorite sexy song.

56

Dirty dancing

Express yourself through dance. Rent the movie *Dirty Dancing* and practice some of those dance moves!

Body language

*E*xpress yourself through sign language. You don't have to learn American Sign Language—just try using gestures to express your sexual desires to your lover. Spend an evening in silence—and, if you can express yourself well enough, spend it in ecstacy!

Dear Diary

*K*eep a "Dirty Diary." Write down all of your fantasies; your daydreams; your sexy dreams; your loving thoughts about your lover; your wishes about what he or she would do with you; your passing sexy thoughts. And then one day, leave your Dirty Diary out where your partner will be sure to come across it.

59
. . .
Lusty poetry

Copy this poem on a piece of parchment paper. Roll it up, tie it with a red ribbon. Leave it on your lover's pillow.

———

"Give me a kiss, and to that kiss a score;
Then to that twenty, add a hundred more:
A thousand to that hundred: so kiss on,
To make that thousand up a million.
Treble that million, and when that is done,
Let's kiss afresh, as when we first begun."

~ Robert Herrick

———

Fantasies

60
· · ·
Welcome to Fantasy Island

*M*any books and "experts" will encourage you to
share your fantasies with your partner. Few of them
will warn you to BE CAREFUL; to tread carefully; to
be sensitive and caring and cautious. While fantasies
are a gateway to sexual fun, they are also a window
into your private, intimate, delicate inner sexual soul.

So move forward, but take it one step at a time.
Respect your partner's sensitivities. And respect your
own Inner Voice. Don't reveal too much too soon—but
do push on your own self-imposed limits occasionally.

Some people are comfortable sharing their sexual fantasies with others—even with strangers. But most of us
are a little more cautious. We need to know and trust
our partner. And even then, it takes us a while. Be
patient with us...because our fantasies are really hot!

You're in good company

$\mathcal{T}$o help you break the ice, let me share with you the results of some sexual surveys that will show that you're in good company:

- Married men and women fantasize about having affairs.
- Many men fantasize about having sex with a prostitute.
- Many women have rape fantasies.
- Most people enjoy having oral sex performed on them, but are a little nervous or reluctant to perform it on their partner.
- Most men love it when women dress up in lingerie for sex.

"How bold one gets when one is sure of being loved."

~ *Sigmund Freud*

62

Focus on your partner

*W*hat erotic fantasies do you have that focus on your partner?

63

Focus on yourself

*W*hat erotic fantasies do you have that focus on you?

64

Photo phantasies

*O*kay, here's a fantasy for you: He pretends he's a *Playboy* photographer, she pretends she's a model.

- Scene 1: He seduces her.
- Scene 2: She seduces him.
- Question: How would the poses be different for *Penthouse?*
- Variation on a theme: She's a *Playgirl* photographer—he's the model.

65

Video fantasies

(See the item above.) Now trade the camera for a video camera. Let your imaginations run wild!

66

Celebrity fantasy

*W*ho is your partner's favorite celebrity? Go out and buy one of those life-sized cardboard stand-up figures. Set it up in your bedroom. Pretend that celebrity is watching your lovemaking session. Or—pretend that you are that celebrity.

67

For marrieds only!

*F*lirt with her at a party, as if you both were single.

- For beginners: Flirt just a little. Wink. Compliment her.
- For intermediate students: Act out a complete

"pick-up" fantasy, without any of the other guests being aware of what you're doing.

- ✦ For advanced students: Continue the fantasy as you return home.
- ✦ For students wanting extra credit: Act out the complete "pick-up" fantasy at the party—and sneak off to an empty room, porch or closet, and make mad, passionate love!

Food, Glorious Food

68
· · ·
Chocolate!

*R*eliable sources report that chocolate may just really be an aphrodisiac.

- ✦ Fact: Chocolate contains large amounts of phenylethylamine, a chemical that is also naturally produced by the body when one is sexually aroused.
- ✦ Fact: The Aztecs considered chocolate to be so powerful a stimulant that women were forbidden from having it!

69
. . .
Tongue twister

69.

70
. . .
Don't cry over spilled wine

$\mathcal{A}$ man in one of my Romance Classes told us how an accidental wine spill resulted in an erotic tradition that he now celebrates regularly with his wife. While dining at home she spilled a glass of wine on her new silk blouse. She looked down at herself and paused. Instead of getting upset, she thought about it for a moment, grabbed *his* wine glass, emptied it down the front of her blouse and said, "If you want it, come and get it!" (They have since graduated to cordials!)

"Life is a banquet and most damned fools are starving to death."

~ Auntie Mame

OMANCE

71

Tom Jones

*R*ent the movie classic *Tom Jones*. Fast forward to the food foreplay scene. Take notes.

72

A good licking

*H*ave you ever covered a portion of your lover's body with food, and then licked it off? (Why not?!?) Try Chocolate sauce, whipped cream, Baileys Irish Cream, honey, butterscotch sauce, jellies and jams.

73
Tasty treats

*B*lindfold your partner. Spread a "mystery flavor" on a private part of your body. Your partner's challenge is to lick it off and name the flavor.

Foreplay

74
Talk, talk, talk

*S*ure, we all know what foreplay is…but have you ever *talked about it* specifically with your partner? You might be surprised to discover that you have different ideas of what it's all about, who should initiate it and how long it should last.

Foreplay, fiveplay, sixplay

$\mathcal{L}$et's define some new terms that may help you get to foreplay!

- ✿ Sevenplay: The shared mindset of a couple who have decided to make love. (You may decide one minute and act on it the next; you may also decide today to make love later in the week.)
- ✿ Sixplay: Clearing away all distractions. Includes telephones, pagers, kids and dogs.
- ✿ Fiveplay: Creating an environment conducive to lovemaking. Includes lighting, music, temperature, comfortable or exciting surroundings.
- ✿ Foreplay: You take it from here...

76
. . .

Before and after

$\mathcal{W}$e're all familiar with foreplay—what we do before getting to the act itself. But what about "postplay"— what we do after the act??

> "A lady always behaves in a manner appropriate to the occasion. The proper behavior for foreplay is unbridled passion, tenderness, eagerness to please, admiration, humor and love.
>
> ~ J, *in* Total Loving

77
. . .
The biggest mistake

- The biggest mistake men tend to make in foreplay is that they don't spend enough time doing it!
- The biggest mistake women tend to make in foreplay is that they are too timid and conservative.

78
. . .
Sexy signals

Create special "signals" to let your lover know you're in the mood for love. Herewith, some ideas from creative Romance Class participants:

- ❧ Have "Your Song" playing on the stereo when he returns home from work.
- ❧ Play anything by Billie Holiday on the stereo.
- ❧ One couple has "His" and "Hers" Japanese kimonos. The interested party changes into his or her robe...and if the other is interested also, he or she changes, too.
- ❧ One couple has an embroidered pillow in their bedroom that says "TONIGHT" on one side, and "NOT TONIGHT" on the other side.

Fun & Games

79
. . .
Spin the bottle

*H*ere's a variation of Spin the Bottle. You take turns spinning a bottle. If it points to your partner, you get to ask him or her to do something sexual

that he or she has never done before. If the bottle
points to you, then you have to do something sexual
that you've never done before.

"Love is being stupid together."

~ *Paul Valery*

80

. . .

Nude Twister???

*H*ere are some game titles. It's *your* job to make up
the rules for them, and then play them with your lover.

- Strip poker
- One-A-Day
- Strip chess
- I Dare You
- Nude Twister
- Don't Stop
- Naughty Charades

- Talk Dirty to Me
- Elevator Challenge
- Taking Turns
- In Public
- Delayed Gratification

81
· · ·
Calendar girl

- Be his "Calendar Girl": Get several photos of yourself blown-up. Then buy a wall calendar for him—replacing some of the calendar photos with your photos! Some suggestions: *The Sports Illustrated Swimsuit Calendar* or *Playboy's Lingerie Calendar.*
- Be her "Calendar Boy": Put your face and your bod on these calendars: The Chippendales Calendar, or any calendar featuring male models.

82
· · ·
Sex toys

- Take the "spinner" from an old board game. Draw a new circle and label it with a dozen sexual activities.

Keep it at your bedside. Take turns giving it a spin and then taking action.

❧ If you want to get really elaborate, take an old board game and create your own "Sexual Monopoly" or "Scrabble Sex" or "The Trivial Pursuit of Sex." Write your own rules. Note: In sex games, even when you lose you win!

83
. . .
Gold, silver, bronze

*H*ow about creating your own private "Sexual Olympics"?! Create a variety of sexual sporting events, "compete" during a two-week period, and award each other bronze, silver and gold medals! Here are some ideas to get you started:

❧ Marathon lovemaking
❧ Floor routines
❧ Marathon oral sex
❧ Orgasm races
❧ Solo stimulation
❧ Mutual stimulation

- Gymnastic sex
- Synchronized orgasms
- Foreplay competition
- Most multiple orgasms

Girl Talk

84

Sex as a competitive sport

*Y*ou know how competitive guys are, right? Well, try tapping into his natural tendency by playing a game of "Sex as a Competitive Sport." Here's how you play. The next time you have sex, you both agree that the goal is for each of you to bring the other to orgasm. The first person to come, loses. (This may be the first game in history in which losing is winning!)

85

Self-exploration

*L*earn as much as you can about your own sexuality. The more you know yourself, your desires, your physical and emotional responses, the more you'll enjoy sex with your partner.

86

Picture this

*E*rotic photographs (also known as "dirty pictures") are a sure turn-on to most men. Flip through a *Playboy* magazine together. Tell him you'd like to get his opinion on which outfits and which poses he finds the most sexy.

87

Miss July

*T*ake action based on the item immediately above! Go shopping to locate that lacy garter belt that Miss

July is wearing! Pose in bed with the photo taped to the headboard.

88

Say "Cheese"!

*H*ow about sexy photos of *you?!* I guarantee he'll love it! You might pose in provocative lingerie—and have a girlfriend take the shots. (You may want to return the favor and photograph her.) Or you may pose in a fantasy outfit, or nude, or draped across his car! For really high quality stuff, hire a professional photographer. (Check references first. And don't worry—real fashion photographers see lots of naked models. It's no big deal to them, and they can help you feel more comfortable.)

89

All dressed up...

*W*hen you're dressed up and out together, secretly hand him your panties under the table. Watch his expression.(If he's not absolutely delighted, he needs help. Serious help.)

90
Flash!
Flash him!

- Secretly dress in a garter belt and stockings…and let him catch a glimpse up your skirt while you're out in public.
- Wear a revealing bra—or none at all and lean over him.

91
Making out

*W*hen's the last time you sat on his lap and "made-out"??

Honeymoon

92
Second honeymoon

*D*ecide to go on a second honeymoon next year. Start

planning and anticipating it now! Buy some books on your destination. Start shopping for your vacation wardrobe this weekend.

93
· · ·

Honeymoon Magazine

Honeymoon Magazine is devoted to helping you plan the most romantic vacation imaginable. Check your local newsstand or call 800-513-7112

—

"A honeymoon is not a place—it's a state of mind."

~ Gregory J.P. Godek

—

94

. . .

Pack your bags

$\mathscr{B}$e prepared to turn any weekend into an "Instant Honeymoon": Have "His" and "Hers" suitcases packed and stored in your car trunk at all times.

95

. . .

Marriage-saver weekends

$\mathscr{T}$ake advantage of nearby hotels' special weekend packages (often called "Marriage-Saver Weekends" or "Lovers' Escape Weekends"). Or find a quaint bed and breakfast or picturesque inn. Pack bags for both of you, and whisk your partner away upon his or her arrival from work!

Hot!

96
. . .
Love & sex

Sometimes love and sex are intertwined—sometimes not.

- Sometimes the deep love, trust and security of a relationship gives sex that extra depth and meaning that propels it into the realm of true ecstasy.
- And other times it's the unique newness of the unknown and strange that makes sex a hot, driving passionate experience.

97
. . .
Notes

The note: "I'm hot for you!" Attach the note to...a pack of matches, a wall thermometer, a bottle of tabasco sauce, a weather report from the newspaper, postcards from the Caribbean, a medical thermometer, a lingerie outfit, a photo of the sun, chili peppers, candles, Fireballs candy!

98

Twice a day??

- ❧ Under what conditions would you…have sex twice in one day?
- ❧ Under what conditions would you…switch sex roles—to the point of dressing in your partner's clothes?
- ❧ Under what conditions would you…pretend to rape (or be raped by) your partner?
- ❧ Under what conditions would you…risk discovery by making love in a quiet corner of a library?

99

Kama Sutra

*G*et a copy of the *Kama Sutra*. Read parts of it aloud to each other. Try some of its suggestions.

100

The Joy of Sex

*G*et a copy of *The Joy of Sex*. Same as above.

> "A kiss can be a comma, a question mark or an exclamation point."
>
> ~ *Mistinguett*

101

Fear of Flying

*R*ead *Fear of Flying,* by Erica Jong. Choose one scene as the inspiration for one of your own fantasies.

102

Kiss, kiss, kiss, kiss, kiss, kiss

*K*iss every square inch of her body…S-L-O-W-L-Y.

103

Good grief!

*F*ind your lover's favorite comic strip in the newspaper. Cut it out. White-out the captions and re-write them—making the characters say some very sexually provocative things! Tape the comic to the bathroom mirror.

Imagination

104

Stop thinking!

*S*ome people just think too much! They've read too many self-help books and sex manuals. Try letting go! Trust your instincts! Don't forget that you have an animal nature inside of you, alongside your human nature.

105

For marrieds only

*T*hink like a single person. Single people are impatient: When they're horny, they act on it!

106

For singles only

*T*hink like a married person. Married people are more concerned with building intimacy than in impressing their partner.

> "People who are sensible about love are incapable of it."
>
> ~ *Douglas Yates*

107
. . .
Aladdin

*B*e a genie: Grant your lover three (sexual) wishes.

108
. . .
Slave to love

*B*e a love slave.

109
. . .
Sex maniac

*B*e an insatiable sex maniac.

110
. . .
Sex coupons

*C*reate your own "Sex Coupons." Write them on 3 x 5
cards or create them on your computer or get custom
certificate forms at a stationery store. Here are a few
ideas to get you started:

- *Sex Slave Coupon*—The issuer of this coupon will be
  the willing (and eager) sex slave of the coupon
  holder for three hours on Saturday.
- *Erotic Massage Coupon*—The coupon holder is
  entitled to a 30-minute erotic massage from the
  coupon issuer.
- *Fantasy Coupon*—This coupon is good for the
  acting-out of the coupon holder's favorite sex
  fantasy.
- *Sex-On-Demand Coupon*—This coupon entitles the
  holder to demand sex from the issuer any time, any
  where during the next year.

111

. . .

Special delivery

$\mathcal{J}$ust imagine…

- 🐾 That he's the sexy UPS delivery man…with a "special delivery" for you.
- 🐾 That you get to re-create your high school prom.
- 🐾 That you meet in a laundromat, having mixed her lingerie with your clothes in the dryer. Sorting them out could lead to…

Le Boudoir

112

. . .

Your sexy hideaway

$\mathcal{T}$he home just may be the least sexy place anywhere. What do you think about when you think of "home"— responsibilities, mom and dad, bills, chores, kids? This is why you need to make your bedroom your private, romantic, sexy hideaway.

113

Once upon a time in Cleveland

- ஃ The scene: An average suburban home in Cleveland.
- ஃ The situation: Husband home alone; wife's gone visiting relatives for two weeks.
- ஃ The Romantic Surprise of the Decade: Husband throws out all bedroom furniture. Wallpapers and refurnishes room. Classic four-poster bed. Antiques.
- ஃ The result: Wife returns home, nearly drops dead of heart attack. Then they try-out the classic four-poster bed—all weekend.

114

Le Boudoir

*Y*our bedroom should be a private, romantic, sexy hideaway. (Get rid of the exercise machine, desk and TV.)

115

Scented sheets

$\mathcal{S}$cent the sheets with perfume or cologne.

116

Recycling rose petals

$\mathcal{S}$prinkle rose petals on the bed.

117

Dim the lights

$\mathcal{S}$oft lighting, please!! Heavy shades, dim bulbs, candles. You want to be able to see what's going on, but you don't need spotlights! (Unless, of course, you're going to be videotaping your lovemaking ...but that's another story!)

118

Mirror, mirror, on the—ceiling?!

$\mathcal{A}$ strategically placed mirror couldn't hurt!

119

Slipping & sliding

*S*atin sheets!

120

Be prepared!

*B*e prepared! Have at bedside:

- Candles
- Erotic literature
- Chocolate tidbits
- Sexy outfits
- Birth control
- Creams & lotions
- Sex toys

121

RVs—"Romance Vehicles"

*H*ow about a "bedroom on wheels"—otherwise known as an RV (Recreational Vehicle—sometimes known as a "Romance Vehicle")?! You can rent one of these things for a few hundred bucks for a few days or weeks, depending on the size of the love-mobile you want. Just think of the possibilities: You can make love at rest stops…Pump each other while pumping gas…And laze away the afternoon in bed regardless of where you are!

122

Hit the bottle

*B*efore you leave on a trip, leave a bottle of massage oil on the night stand, along with a note: "To be used on you upon my return."

Lingerie

123

Just what is Victoria's secret?!

*N*eedless to say, "Victoria's Secret" has become synonymous with "Lingerie" in the minds of modern

Americans. Their lingerie selection is exquisite; the stores are a sensual experience; and the catalog is the most awaited piece of mail that most of us receive!

124
A wild goose chase

$\mathcal{T}$om arrived home from running some errands one Saturday morning to find his wife, Susan, gone. He found a note that said, "Go to the mall. Go to the Information Desk. Ask for me there." Puzzled but curious, Tom went to the mall.

At the Information Desk they gave him a sealed envelope. The note inside said: "Proceed to Victoria's Secret. Ask for me there." Puzzled but excited, Tom made his way to Victoria's Secret. They had a wrapped package waiting for him there. The note on it said: "No peeking! Now, proceed to 4128 Maple Street. Ask for me there." Puzzled and even more excited, Tom made his way there. It turned out to be a romantic bed and breakfast, where he finally found his wife.

125
Playboy

*H*ave you ever noticed that there really aren't many naked women in *Playboy*? They're almost always wearing something—usually something lacy, skimpy and satiny. Think about it.

126
Dressing room delight

*G*o lingerie shopping together. Join her in the dressing room.

127
A budget for bras

*M*ake a special item on your yearly household budget for lingerie. Go shopping every other month for new stuff! (This trip she chooses what she wants. Next trip he chooses what he wants.)

128

. . .

Guys...

*G*uys: When you buy lingerie for her, don't just buy one item—put together matching outfits: bra, panties, garter belt, stockings. Or maybe a lacy teddy with matching tap pants.

129

. . .

Gals...

*G*als: When you buy lingerie, don't just *show* it to him—*model it* for him! (Draw the curtains and model for him in the kitchen or family room! Lingerie needn't be confined to the bedroom!)

130

. . .

Panty-of-the-Month Club

*U*se your imagination: Create your own "Panty-of-the-Month Club"!

131

Special delivery

- Mail one item of your sexiest lingerie to him at work!
- Mail an entire outfit to him—one piece per day for a whole week!
- Include a note describing (in explicit detail) how you're going to model it for him tonight.

132

Catalog corner

For those of you who are a bit timid about walking into a lingerie shop, here's help from a few catalogs:

- Victoria's Secret—800-888-8200
- Playboy—800-423-9494
- Frederick's of Hollywood—800-323-9525
- Dream Dresser—800-963-7326
- Barely Nothings—800-4-BARELY
- Maitresse—800-456-8464
- Fashion Fantasies—800-858-0565

133

Lingerie fashion show

- How about staging a personal Lingerie Fashion Show for him?
- Or how about creating a Lingerie Fashion Show *videotape* for him?!

Lovemaking

134

One part sex, one part love

Take a little sex, stir-in a generous portion of love, and you get—lovemaking. Let's take a moment to appreciate this unique and wonderfully human creation. It's an incredible melding of our animal nature and our spiritual nature.

135

Looking for clues

- Pay close attention to your lover's breathing patterns during lovemaking.
- Listen to the noises she makes as she's aroused.
- Notice the muscle tone of your lover's body during different phases of your lovemaking.

What's the difference between "having sex" and "making love"?

136

Use your imagination

*H*ow many different kinds of lovemaking can you think of?

- Planned or spontaneous
- Loud or quiet

- Indoors or outdoors
- Clothed or naked
- Slow or fast
- Fantasy or kinky

Variety

Try these ideas on for size. How do they fit for you? What turns you on? What turns you off? Share this information with your lover!

137
. . .
Shut-eye

Make love with your eyes closed.

138

Shhh!

*M*ake love without uttering a word.

139

Pillow talk

*M*ake love, talking softly throughout.

140

That's what zippers are for

*M*ake love fully clothed.

141
. . .
Props

*H*ow could you use these items as part of your love-making?

- ❧ Three pillows
- ❧ Baileys Irish Cream
- ❧ A silk tie or scarf
- ❧ Chocolate pudding
- ❧ Silk stockings (black, seamed)
- ❧ A blindfold
- ❧ A video camera
- ❧ Two ice cubes
- ❧ A feather
- ❧ Rose petals
- ❧ 100 candles
- ❧ A mirror
- ❧ Your car

142
. . .
Bubblebaths

*B*e waiting for him in the bathtub when he returns from work.

143

Bathroom bopping

$\mathcal{T}$est your agility—make love in the bathtub. If your tub is simply too small, spread towels on the floor and improvise!

"He who is not impatient is not in love."

~ Italian proverb

Mindset of a Sex Maniac

144

Questions

$\mathcal{H}$ow do you think about sex? Do you think about it differently at different times? Do you ever talk about this aspect of sex with your partner?

- ❧ Is sex a physical release?
- ❧ Is sex a form of communication?
- ❧ Is sex a form a competition?
- ❧ Are things communicated through sex that you can't say any other way?
- ❧ Is sex an obligation?
- ❧ Is sex the most fun a person can have?

145

Bartering

*S*ex maniacs will do nearly anything to have sex. Even barter favors for it! Try this game with your partner: Trade sex for various activities or favors or chores that your partner really, really wants. You might trade oral sex for cleaning out the garage. Or trade acting out a fantasy for a favorite meal. Or trade a long, sensuous massage for babysitting the kids.

146

Anticipation

𝒢uys: Call her at work (or from work), and tell her that you've just purchased a pair of silk boxer shorts; that they're her favorite color; that you're wearing them right now; and that you're going to model them for her this evening.

147

In public?!?

𝒲hile out in public—at a party, walking down the street—lean over and whisper something outrageously sexy in his or her ear. Be specific. Be graphic. Then continue on your way.

148
. . .
Weird Science

*H*ave you ever seen the movie *Weird Science*? It's about these two guys who create a woman. Turns out she has a mind of her own (imagine that!!) and things get out of hand and they have all kinds of crazy adventures. What does this have to do with your sex life? Well, here are some fantasies based on *Weird Science:*

- He creates her. She has a mind of her own. Wild sex ensues!
- He creates her. She is obedient and will do anything he asks.
- She creates *him!*

149
. . .
Urges

*H*ave you ever been out in public with your partner, and had a sudden urge to take him or her right then and there? What prevented you? Make yourself a promise to act on the urge the next time it happens.

How do you balance sex and love?
Giving and taking?
Control and letting go?

Sexy Stuff

150

Myths and other fallacies

- ❧ "Nice girls don't enjoy sex much." Nice girls love sex—they just don't blab about it!
- ❧ "I shouldn't have to ask my lover for what I want." Sorry, but most of us aren't mindreaders. Ask and ye shall receive!

151

On the floor

𝒜 sheepskin rug.

152
· · ·
Sexy supplies

- ✿ A bottle of massage oil.
- ✿ Bubblebath powder.
- ✿ His favorite perfume. Her favorite cologne.

153
· · ·
Sexy flowers

*F*lowers may be romantic, but can they be *sexy*?? You bet! Send her an arrangement with Paphiopedilum orchids or Birds of Paradise!

154
· · ·
Horny feelings on paper

*W*rite a quick, sexy note to your lover. (Just do it! No excuses.) We're not striving for eloquence here—merely some hot thoughts, lusty ideas, sexy suggestions.

155

Sex vs. television

*H*ave sex instead of watching TV tonight.

156

Aaaaahhhhh

*F*ill a basin with hot water. Take off her shoes for her.
Sit her down in her favorite chair. Wash her feet.
Massage them in hot, soapy water. Let her feet soak
for 10 minutes. Dry them off. Rub lotion on her feet.
Aaaah!

157

Singing of sex

*W*rite a song about the most spectacular sex you've
experienced with your partner. Now, sing it to him!

158
. . .
Words of sex

*W*rite a poem in praise of your lover's sexiest body part.

159
. . .
A sexy wake-up call

*W*hen he's traveling on business, call him at his hotel room and give him a sexy wake-up call!

160
. . .
Massage

*D*on't forget that massages come in two varieties: sensual and sexual. Learn the subtle—but important—differences. One will relax your partner and put her to sleep. The other is, essentially, foreplay.

Orgasm

161

. . .

Hmmmmm

*H*um while you're performing oral sex on your partner!

162

. . .

Positioning

*V*ariety is the spice of life, they say. How many different positions do you have in your repertoire of lovemaking techniques? Most people settle on one or two positions and rarely experiment.

> "The potion drunk by lovers is prepared by no one but themselves. The potion is the sum of one's whole existence."
>
> ~ *Anais Nin*

163
· · ·
Summer camp

*W*hat does summer camp have to do with orgasms? From a reader: "Summer camp allows us to reclaim our house from our children. It's so nice to have LOUD orgasms for two weeks out of the year!"

164
· · ·
Peek-a-boo!

*D*o you tend to have orgasm with your eyes open or closed? Next time, try it the opposite way, just to experience what it's like.

Outrageous

165

Keep an open mind

$\mathcal{I}$'m a bit leery about using the word "outrageous"—because something that is easy and natural to one person may be outrageous and kinky to another person, and may be distasteful and threatening to a third person. So let's keep an open mind and see what happens...

166

Flying solo

$\mathcal{A}$re you comfortable enough with each other to masturbate in the other's presence? (You could learn a lot about how to please your partner.)

167

Tying the knot

Scarves and ties and ropes, oh my! Have you ever wanted to make love while being bound? Have you ever wanted to tie-up your lover? Kinky? Perhaps. But lots of people say it's a great turn-on!

"The loving are the daring."

~ *Bayard Taylor*

168

Skinny-dipping

Go skinny-dipping. In a river. In an ocean. In a pond. In your neighbor's pool.

169

All-nighter

*S*tay up all night talking and making love and talking and making love and eating and making love and watching old movies and making love and making love.

170

Favorite fantasies

*W*hat's your favorite sexual fantasy? Have you ever described it to your lover?

171

Building your vocabulary

*O*pen a dictionary to any page. At random, point to a word. You and your lover must figure out some way to include that word, idea or concept into your lovemaking some time in the next week.

172

Seduction

Seduce your partner while you're watching TV together. (Set the VCR to tape the show you're watching so he won't have any excuse not to join in the fun!)

173

Role playing

Characters and roles to consider for your fantasies.

- Teacher
- Prostitute
- Pilot
- Stewardess
- Doctor
- Nurse
- Cowboy
- Model
- Playmate
- Neighbor
- Boss
- Secretary

- Geisha girl
- Masseuse
- Therapist
- Babysitter

(What secret fantasies have you kept deep inside? You have nothing to lose but your inhibitions, and lots to gain!)

Questions

174
. . .
Q&A

- If he were Prince Charming, how would he make love with you?
- If she were a high class escort, what sexual favors would she perform?
- If you were going to write and direct an erotic movie, what would its title be? Who would star in it? What's the plot?

- If money were no object, where would you go to have sex?
- If money were no object, how would you dress you and your partner for sex?
- If you could hypnotize your partner and ask him or her to perform any sex act with you, what would it be?

"No man really becomes a fool until he stops asking questions."

~ *Charles Proteus Steinmitz*

175
· · ·
Who? What? When?

- What prevents you from sharing your fantasies with your partner?
- What do you do when you're sexually frustrated?
- What foreplay activity do you most enjoy

performing for your lover?

- ❧ What foreplay activity do you most enjoy having performed for you?
- ❧ What grade would you give yourself as a lover? (Grade yourself like in school: A through F.) What grade would you give your partner?
- ❧ What would you like to ask your partner that you've always felt uncomfortable asking?

176
. . .
Why?

- ❧ How often would you like to have sex?
- ❧ How would your sex life be different if you were the last two people on earth?
- ❧ How do you like to be fondled? (Be specific.)

177
. . .
Where? How?

- ❧ What does an orgasm look like? (What color is it? Does it tingle, explode, flow? Does it linger? How long?) How else would you describe an orgasm? What does your partner's orgasm look like??
- ❧ What is a spouse's obligation to have sex with his or her mate?

Role Playing

Here are some ideas for roles you might play during your fantasies...

178
· · ·
Just do it

*F*antasizing, role playing, sex play...What does it all mean? What is the deeper significance? Do our desires signal deep neurosis? Do our fantasies reveal suppressed feelings? Possibly, probably—and *so what?!?* There's a time and a place for deep psychological analysis. But I don't think we need to drag our therapists into bed with us all the time.

179
· · ·
School daze

More fantasy roles for you to consider...

- ✬ She's a cheerleader (sexy but innocent). He's a football player (confident and horny).

- She's a cheerleader (the school sexpot). He's a math nerd (handsome but inexperienced).
- She's a teacher. He's a student. (She seduces him.)
- She's a teacher. He's a student. (He seduces her.)
- He's the teacher. (You know what to do.)

180
. . .
Playing doctor

- He's a doctor. She's a patient. (He seduces her.)
- He's a doctor. She's a patient. (She seduces him.)
- She's a doctor. He's a patient. (She seduces him.)
- She's a doctor. He's a patient. (He seduces her.)
- She's a nurse. He's a doctor.
- She's a nurse. He's a patient.
- Dentist. Intern. Candystriper!

181
. . .
9 to 5

- She's the boss (horny). He's the mail boy (unsuspecting).

Romantic Fantasies

- He's the boss (horny). She's the secretary (demure).
- He's the boss (unsuspecting). She's the secretary (outrageous!).
- She's interviewing him for a job.
- She works in a lingerie shop. He's shopping.
- She's a high class "escort."
- He's a young gigolo.

182
. . .
Here, there, everywhere

*A*nd here are some fantasy roles focusing on different places...

- You're at an out-of-town convention.
- You're out camping.
- One of you is a lifeguard who saves the other's life.
- You're at a bar. One of you is the bartender.

Seduction

183
· · ·
Do it up right

*W*hen's the last time you seduced your spouse? How often do you bother to "set the mood," play the music, dress the part, say the right words, do the little things?

184
· · ·
Shower power

*B*egin your seduction in the shower. Lather your partner. Take your time. Towel her off. Gently.

Sex in the Movies

185
· · ·
"His" and "Hers"

*W*hen choosing erotic movies…it may be helpful to

remember that men and women often have different definitions of "erotic." Women tend to like the smoldering passion of *The Bridges of Madison County.* For men, you can pretty much sum up their taste in erotic movies in two words: "Nude blonde." *(Basic Instinct, Nine-1/2 Weeks, Body Double.)*

186
· · ·
Acting out

*A*ct out a favorite scene from a favorite sexy movie. (You choose the movie this week, your partner chooses the movie next week.)

187
· · ·
For your consideration

- Nine-1/2 Weeks
- Body Heat
- The Big Easy

- Henry and June
- The Lovers
- Sea of Love
- Wild Orchid

188

Blinded by love

Blindfold her. Sit her on the floor next to the refrigerator. Feed her a variety of delicious foods: Strawberries, cherry tomatoes, Hershey's Kisses, cheese, ice cream, Cheerios, cookies, popcorn, yogurt, watermelon, leftover chicken, pickles, olives, maple syrup, etc. (Inspired by a great scene in the movie *Nine-1/2 Weeks.*)

189

From Here to Eternity

- *From Here to Eternity*...the classic from 1953, when films weren't quite so graphic...and yet, that love scene on the beach amid the ocean waves...

Sex, Sex, Sex

190
· · ·
50/50

*W*hen you make love, is it a 50/50 proposition? Is it an equal opportunity experience? Do you take turns? Is it fairly balanced? Do you both get your sexual needs met? Sometimes 80/20 is okay, as when one of you decides to pleasure the other, while putting your needs on hold.

191
· · ·
Questions

*W*ho initiates sex? Who communicates more? Who touches more? Who comes first?

192
· · ·
Homework

*G*rab a pad and pen. List all of the reasons you and

your partner have for not having sex as often as you'd like. Don't hold anything back. List everything. Discuss your lists together. I'll be honest with you: You'll probably get into a fight over this. That's okay. Why? Because we often have to clear away the past before we can move forward.

"Sex alleviates tension. Love causes it."

~ Woody Allen

193

Love Nest

Create a "Love Nest"—right in the middle of your living room. Picture the scene: He comes home from work; it's dark. He tries to turn on the light—but you've pulled the fuses. There are candles leading him into the living room...where you're sprawled out on the floor...amid a mountain of pillows...provocatively dressed...moving to the beat of soft, erotic music...with champagne at hand...

194

Create a "Love Nest"

How would you create a "Love Nest" in your car? In your office? In a suitcase—for roving romantics! In your attic?

195

Imagination

*E*nroll your partner in the "Fantasy of the Month Club." You make up the rules for the club. Let your imagination run wild!

196

Libido Magazine

Armchair lovers might prefer their erotica at home and in prose. You might consider subscribing to *Libido Magazine*—"Erotica for people who like to read." Write to P.O. Box 146721, Chicago, Illinois 60614.

197

Location, location, location

Have you fantasized about making love somewhere where you've never done it before?

- In a limousine
- On horseback
- In a Victoria's Secret dressing room
- In the back seat of the car
- In the front seat of the car—while he's driving!
- On a plane in your seats under a blanket
- On a plane or train, in the restroom
- In an elevator
- In her office on her desk
- At the top of a ferris wheel

- In a hammock
- In a church
- On the steps of the Lincoln Memorial in Washington, D.C.
- In a movie theater—during the movie
- In France—anywhere, just so it's in France
- In front of the window of a hotel room in Manhattan—where office workers could potentially see you!

Sexy Songs

198
. . .
Choreography

"Choreograph" your lovemaking to your favorite music! I don't mean that you plan every movement, but rather that you match some favorite music to the general mood and pace of your lovemaking.

- For example, some people like to start slowly and gently, and build to a fast-paced climax. (Pun intended.) Their musical choreography could look like this: start with a little George Winston; move to some Al Jarreau; mix-in some Benny Goodman; and finish-up with Maynard Ferguson.

❧ Others like to start-out fast and passionately, and wind-down to a gentle conclusion. Their musical choreography could look like this: start with the soundtrack from Nine-1/2 Weeks; move to the soundtrack from When Harry Met Sally; and end with the soundtrack from Out of Africa.

❧ One couple from New Jersey prefers Mozart symphonies. They suggest The Jupiter Symphony, No. 41. "It has four movements, which correspond with our pattern of lovemaking: 1) The first movement is strong and passionate, which gets us going; and it runs 11:50—good for energetic foreplay. 2) The second movement slows the pace, which allows us to talk a little and build the intimacy more. 3) The third movement picks up the speed again, which moves us from quiet intimacy into a more intense passion. 4) The last movement races to a roaring and passionate conclusion."

199

Striptease

*P*erform a striptease for your partner.

- Practice first! Rent some movies with stripping scenes to get some choreography ideas. *(Nine-1/2 Weeks, Striptease.)*
- Select a song that will get both of you hot and bothered. ("You Can Leave your Hat On," by Joe Cocker; "Principles of Lust" by Enigma.)
- Note: Stripping isn't just for women. C'mon guys…let's see if you have the confidence to be your honey's very own Chippendale!

200

Mood music

- "My Old Flame" by Billie Holiday.
- "Rhythm of the Heat" by Peter Gabriel.
- "I Want Your Sex" by George Michael.

More Sexy Stuff

201
. . .

Adventure #1: Beach Party Rendezvous

- Music: Beach Boys, Monkees
- Movies: Beach Blanket Bingo, all those Annette Funicelo movies
- Food: Grilled burgers, chips
- Drink: Beer
- Dress: Swimming trunks & bikinis
- Props: Cool sunglasses, sand, beach balls, Coppertone
- Fantasy #1: One of you, as a lifeguard, seduces the other
- Fantasy #2: "Baywatch"
- Fantasy #3: As strangers, you rub lotion on her back, leading to...

202
. . .

Adventure #2: 1950s Nostalgia

- Music: Elvis, The Four Freshmen, Buddy Holly

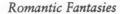

- Movies: Picnic, Grease, Elvis movies
- Food: Burgers, onion rings, diner food, Jello
- Dress: Bobbie socks & saddle shoes, poodle skirts, Varsity sweaters
- Props: A '57 Chevy, horn rimmed glasses
- Fantasy #1: A date as innocent teenagers who stumble into sex
- Fantasy #2: A necking session in the back seat gets out of hand!
- Fantasy #3: After school, you're studying together, and...

203
. . .

Adventure #3: Sex, Sex, Sex!

- Music: Eurhythmics, Nine-1/2 Weeks soundtrack, Sade
- Movies: Emmanuel, Body Heat, Nine-1/2 Weeks
- Food: Smoked oysters, Godiva Chocolates
- Drink: Champagne
- Dress: Optional
- Props: According to your particular liking or fetish!

& Other Sexy Ways of Expressing Your Love

- Fantasy #1: Pure, lustful, rip-each-other's-clothes-off sex!
- Fantasy #2: Watch an erotic movie; act-out a favorite scene
- Fantasy #3: Tease one another for as long as you can stand it!

204

Adventure #4: An Evening of Romance & Sex

- Music: Glenn Miller, George Benson, George Winston
- Movies: Casablanca, Ghost, West Side Story, any Fred Astaire movie
- Food: French bread & cheese
- Drink: the most expensive champagne you can afford
- Dress: Tuxedo & evening gown
- Props: Candles, red roses, crystal champagne flutes
- Fantasy #1: Romance each other for one hour before making love
- Fantasy #2: You're strangers who meet at a friend's wedding...
- Fantasy #3: Make love with you clothes on

Taking Care of Business

205
· · ·
I ♥ NY

Perhaps a little travel might inspire your libido. You might want to visit:

- ॐ Love, Arizona
- ॐ Eros, Arkansas
- ॐ Goodnight, Colorado
- ॐ Pleasure Beach, Connecticut
- ॐ Venus, Florida
- ॐ Bliss, Idaho
- ॐ Lovejoy, Illinois
- ॐ Loveland, Iowa
- ॐ Ogle, Kentucky
- ॐ Union, Maine
- ॐ Romeo, Michigan
- ॐ Darling, Minnesota
- ॐ Bond, Mississippi
- ॐ Valentine, Montana
- ॐ Sparks, Nebraska
- ॐ Loving, New Mexico

- Intercourse, Pennsylvania
- Sweet Lips, Tennessee
- Eureka, Texas
- Paradise, Utah
- Casanova, Virginia
- Romance, West Virginia

—and—

There are towns named Climax in Colorado, Kansas, Minnesota, New Mexico, New York, North Carolina, Ohio, Pennsylvania, and (not to be left out)...Texas.

206

Lunch date

Make a lunch date with your partner. Bring a picnic basket to her office. The picnic basket is filled with blankets and pillows. Make love on her desk. (Lock the door and hold all calls!)

"The meeting of two personalities is like the contact of two chemical substances: if there is any reaction both are transformed."

~ Carl G. Jung

207

Meet after work

*M*eet after work at a local hotel for drinks. Surprise her by having a room reserved. Spend the night pretending you're having an affair.

208

...

B&B

*P*lan a three-day weekend at a romantic bed and breakfast. Tell her you'll make all the arrangements and pack the bags. Bring an empty suitcase for her—and don't let her discover it until you arrive at the inn. Tell her she simply won't be needing any clothing; then make good on that promise!

209

...

Pick a card, any card

*M*ake a "Sex Jar": Write sexual activities, ideas and fantasies on 100 small cards. Put them in an old cookie jar. Choose one card a week and follow its instructions! (Or you could simply number hundreds of small slips of paper, and refer to the corresponding number in this book! You could take turns reaching into the jar: your turn this week, his turn next week.)

Time for Sex

210
· · ·
12 months of loving

*E*ach month, subtly focus on a different part of her body. Give her massages; stroke her; buy her little gifts for that part of her body. See how long it takes her to notice. (No, you can't start with her breasts. Geez, you guys—show a little class—exercise a little restraint!) Hands, feet, face, hair, back, legs, shoulders, neck, ears, head, etc.

211
· · ·
Questions

- On a scale of 1 to 10, how important is sex to you?
- On a scale of 1 to 10, how "normal" sexually do you think you are?
- On a scale of 1 to 10, how creative are you in your lovemaking?

What a week!

$\mathcal{C}$hoose a week, and give yourself permission to think about sex all the time. (You probably do anyway, but you may feel somewhat guilty about it.) Don't forget to give your partner permission, too!

"Sexuality is not a leisure or part-time activity. It is a way of being."

~ Alexander Lowen

213

A week of sex

- ❧ Sunday—Read the Sunday newspapers in bed. Stay in bed all day.
- ❧ Monday—Whoever wakes up first gets to wake the other—by kissing the other's genitals.

- Tuesday—Sex before sunrise!
- Wednesday—Sex *after* sunset!
- Thursday—Phone sex at noon.
- Friday—Meet after work for a movie date. Make out in the theater.
- Saturday—Go for a drive. Find a secluded spot. Make love in the back seat.

214
. . .
Leno vs. sex vs. Letterman

*D*on't leave lovemaking until just before sleeping! Why is it so often the last item on the list? (Why do so many people have their priorities so screwed-up?? How could those silly household chores possibly be more important than making love with your partner?)

215
. . .
Get up!

$\mathcal{M}$ake time in the morning to make love. Get up an hour earlier!

216
. . .
A year of sex

- January—Make a New Year's resolution to make love once a week.
- February—Don't wait for Valentine's Day, start celebrating on the 1st!
- March—Let's declare March to be National Lingerie Month. I'd say that one new outfit per week should be a minimum requirement!
- April—Let's declare April to be National Women's Sexuality Month. Learn more about her sexuality; put her needs first—all month!
- May—Seems only fair that May should be National Men's Sexuality Month.
- June—Focus on the more *romantic* aspects of sex in June.

- July—Create a month of sexual fireworks, starting on the 4th.
- August—August is a hot month anyway, so dedicate this month to the hottest sex of the year.
- September—September means "back to school"—so dedicate this month to learning more about your sexuality.
- October—Focus on the outrageous/wild/kinky side of sex this month.
- November—Focus on the visual side of sex this month.
- December—Create your own "Twelve Days of Sex" based on the song "The Twelve Days of Christmas"!

ABCs of Sex

217
· · ·

Do you know your ABCs?

Ask your partner to pick a letter. Then read the list of corresponding words. He or she has 24 hours in which to get a sexy gift or perform an erotic gesture based on any one of the key words.

- A is for Ardor, Aphrodisiacs, Ardent, Attitude, Australia, Available.
- B is for Boudoir, B&B, Beaches, Brandy, Bubblebaths, Bahamas.
- C is for Cunnilingus, Champagne, Candlelight, Chocolate, Convertible.
- D is for Dirty Dancing, Dating, Dinner, Dating, Diamonds.
- E is for Erotic, Exotic, Elvis, Excitement, Enthusiasm, Escape.
- F is for Fellatio, Foreplay, Fantasies, France, Frenching, Flowers.
- G is for G-Spot, Garters, Godiva, Gifts.
- H is for Honeymoons, Humor, Hugs, Hide-Aways.
- I is for Intrigue, Intimacy, Imagination, Inns, Islands, Incense, Italy.
- J is for Jazz, Jacuzzi, Jewelry, Jello.
- K is for Kinky, Kissing.
- L is for Lingerie, Laughing, Leather, Lace, Limousines, Lovemaking.
- M is for Mistletoe, Masculine, Movies, Massage.
- N is for Naughty, Nibble, Nubile, Nymph, Negligee, Nighttime.

- O is for Orgasm, Outrageous, Outdoors.
- P is for Panties, Passion, Perfume, Poetry, Paris, Playfulness.
- Q is for Quiet, Quaint, Queen, Quebec, QE2.
- R is for Rendezvous, Roses, Rituals, Rapture, Rope, Red.
- S is for Sex.
- T is for Teasing, Titillating, Toys, Theater, Togetherness, Talking.
- U is for Undress, Undulate, Urges, Unexpected, Union.
- V is for Virgins, Vibrators, Venice, Venus, Valentines, Victoria's Secret.
- W is for Wine, Weddings, Wench, Weird.
- X is for X-Rated, Xerox, Xmas.
- Y is for Yes, Yachts, Yin & Yang, Young-at-heart.
- Z is for Zany, Zeal, Zodiac.

Romantic Fantasies

For a free one-year subscription to Greg Godek's
LoveLetter Newsletter send your name and address to:

LoveLetter
Sourcebooks
P.O. Box 372
Naperville, IL 60566

Would you like to see your name in print in a future
book?! If you have a romantic, creative or outrageous
story that you would like to share, please send it to:

Love Stories
Sourcebooks
P.O. Box 372
Naperville, IL 60566

Would you be interested in having Greg Godek present
a speech or seminar to your group?

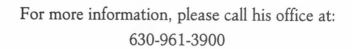

For more information, please call his office at:
630-961-3900

Other books in this series include:

Romantic Dates: Ways to Woo & Wow the One You Love
ISBN: 1-57071-153-4; $6.95

Romantic Mischief: The Playful Side of Love
ISBN: 1-57071-151-8; $6.95

Romantic Questions: Growing Closer Through
Intimate Conversation
ISBN: 1-57071-152-6; $6.95

Also by Gregory J.P. Godek

1001 Ways to Be Romantic
5th Anniversary Edition of the Bestselling Classic!
ISBN: 1-883518-05-9; $14.95

1001 More Ways to Be Romantic
ISBN: 0-9629803-2-3; $11.95

To order these books or any other of our many publications, please contact your local bookseller, gift store or call Sourcebooks. Books by Gregory J.P. Godek are available in book and gift stores across North America. Get a copy of our catalog by writing or faxing:

Sourcebooks
P. O. Box 372
Naperville, IL 60566
(630) 961-3900
FAX: (630) 961-2168